22009

PLATE TECTONICS

ALVIN SILVERSTEIN · VIRGINIA SILVERSTEIN · LAURA SILVERSTEIN NUNN

TWENTY-FIRST CENTURY BOOKS
BROOKFIELD, CONNECTICUT

Cover photograph courtesy of Photo Researchers (© E. R. Degginger)

Photographs courtesy of Corbis: p. 4; The Granger Collection, New York: pp. 6, 47; U. S. Geological Survey: pp. 7 (J. K. Nakata), 8, 14, 22, 44; Alfred Wegener Institute for Polar Marine Research: p. 13; Woods Hole Oceanographic Institution: pp. 18, 45 (© Jack Cook); Nordic Volcanological Institute (Gigir Vid Sandmula): p. 23; NOAA: pp. 12, 37; Icelandic Tourist Board: pp. 25, 53; Photo Researchers: p. 27 (© Martin Bond/Science Photo Library), 40 (© Jim Corwin), 48 (© Russell D. Curtis); © Archive Photos: p. 33; Woodfin Camp & Associates: p. 39 (© A. Ramey); Reuters/Corbis-Bettmann: p. 42; Science Museum/Science & Society Picture Library: p. 49; NASA: p. 54
Diagrams by XNR Productions

Library of Congress Cataloging-in-Publication Data

Silverstein, Alvin.
Plate tectonics / Alvin and Virginia Silverstein and Laura Silverstein Nunn.
p.   cm. — (Science concepts)
Includes bibliographical references and index.
Summary: Discusses plate tectonics, the theory that the surface
of the earth is always moving, and the connection of this
phenomenon to earthquakes and volcanoes.

ISBN 0-7613-3225-1 (lib. bdg.)
1. Plate tectonics—Juvenile literature. [1. Plate tectonics. 2. Earthquakes.
3. Volcanoes.] I. Silverstein, Virginia B. II. Nunn, Laura Silverstein.
III. Title. IV. Series: Silverstein, Alvin. Science concepts.

QF511.4.S55   1998
555.1'36—dc21   98-24934
                                                                     CIP
                                                                     AC

Published by Twenty-First Century Books
A Division of The Millbrook Press, Inc.
2 Old New Milford Road
Brookfield, Connecticut 06804

CONTENTS

Earthquake aftermath. On the Bay Bridge, which connects San Francisco and Oakland, Linda Reed scans the collapsed section to see if her husband was trapped. Fortunately, he wasn't.

Our Planet Earth

We usually think of the ground under our feet as firm and solid, but it is not always so. During an **earthquake** the ground trembles and shakes. The most violent earthquakes can send huge buildings crashing down and crumple bridges and superhighways. When a **volcano** erupts, a formerly quiet mountain begins to rumble and smoke, then literally blows its top. A cloud of hot ash spews out, and burning-hot **lava**—melted rock—pours down the mountainside, destroying everything in its path.

Much slower changes also occur on our not-so-quiet planet earth. Huge mountain ranges thrust up in places where there have been only flatlands or even sea bottoms. Other mountains are gradually wearing away.

Early humans wondered about their world and its mysteries. What enormous forces could make the solid ground shake and even split apart? What could make a peaceful mountain turn into an erupting volcano? People made up myths, or stories, to explain the workings of the world. Hindus in ancient India believed that the earth was as flat as a dinner plate and rested on the backs of four elephants standing on the shell of a giant turtle. According to a Japanese myth, a giant catfish lived deep inside the earth. Sometimes it thrashed about violently, causing an earthquake.

It was not until the twentieth century that a scientific theory was finally worked out to explain earthquakes, volcanoes, and many other puzzles of our planet. This is the plate tectonic theory. In order to understand it, we first need to learn a few things about our planet earth.

By the sixth century B.C., Greek scientists had figured out that the earth was round, like a ball. They thought, however, that it was a solid ball located at the center of the universe.

Beginning in the late fifteenth century, as explorers discovered and mapped more of the world, people were impressed with the huge oceans and wondered where all the water had come from. They thought perhaps the solid part of the earth was just an outer crust, enclosing an inside filled with water. Erupting volcanoes, however, suggested that the inside of the earth contained fiery-hot melted rock.

Ancient Greek conception of universe as depicted in an engraving made in Amsterdam, the Netherlands, in 1660.

By the late 1800s, most **geologists** (scientists who study the earth) agreed on the following: The earth most likely has a solid inner **core** made of heavy metals; an outer **crust** of rock; and hot melted rock in between. The liquid part, called the **mantle**, is kept constantly churning by currents produced by the heat of the core. At times, some of the mantle material bursts out through weak spots in the crust, such as when a volcano erupts.

Scientists studying earthquakes later obtained evidence supporting these ideas about the earth's structure. An instrument called a **seismograph**, developed in 1880, measures the waves of energy transmitted through the earth during a quake. Like light rays passing from air through a glass of water, the **seismic waves** of an earthquake bend slightly as they go from one material to another. The seismograph records show a bend about 20–45 miles (32–72 km) down from the earth's surface, marking the boundary between the solid crust and the mantle. Another bend much farther down toward the center of the earth marks the boundary between the mantle and the core.

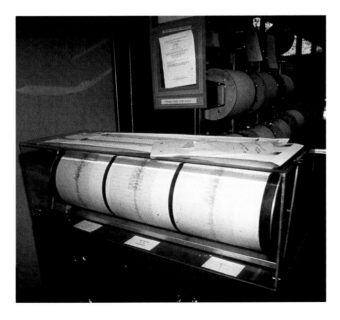

Seismographs at the U.S. Geological Survey record the north-south horizontal, east-west horizontal and vertical components of the October 17, 1989, California earthquake.

The core actually consists of two separate layers. The inner core is a solid ball of iron and nickel, about 1,500 miles (2,400 km) in diameter. It is very dense and is under enormous pressure—3.6 million times the pressure at the earth's surface. The inner core is also extremely hot—more than 10,000°F (nearly 6,000°C), as hot as the surface of the sun. A liquid outer core surrounds the inner core. It is believed to be made up mostly of molten iron, with small amounts of other elements such as silicon, sulfur, and oxygen. This hot liquid part of the core is about 1,400 miles (2,250 km) thick.

The mantle that surrounds the outer core extends almost to the surface of the earth. It is about 1,800 miles (2,900 km) thick and is composed of various rocky materials. The mantle is actually solid, but under slow, gradual pressure it can flow like a thick liquid. (Think of mud.) The pressure is highest in the lower mantle, and rocks that float down from the upper mantle become much denser.

In the upper mantle hot rocks melt into a liquid called **magma**.

The crust, the outermost layer, is not the same thickness all over the earth's surface. Under the oceans it is rather thin, in some places less than 4 miles (6 km) thick. It is also dense, made of rock called basalt. The **continents** (the landmasses) are formed by thicker parts of the crust—

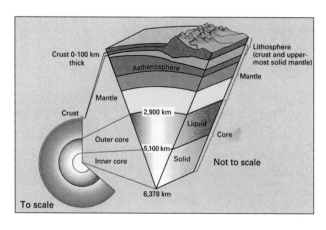

This section of the earth shows its layers.

from about 16 miles (about 25 km) thick at the coasts, to 20–25 miles (about 30–40 km) thick under the plains and deserts, to as high as 56 miles (90 km) under the highest mountain ranges. Even the "thin" parts of the earth's crust are not very thin compared to the distances we usually deal with. The deepest mine in the world is less than 2.5 miles (4 km) deep, and the deepest holes ever drilled went down about 9 miles (15 km).

✦ ARMOR-PLATED EARTH ✦

A number of deep cracks in the crust extend into the upper mantle. These form the outlines of large masses of rock, known as **tectonic plates**. (*Tecton* is the Greek word for "builder.") The earth's outer shell is made up of about a dozen large plates and a number of smaller ones, fitted together like the parts of a jigsaw puzzle. The plates are about 30 to 50 miles (50 to 80 km) thick, and some are huge compared with others. The whole North American continent, together with part of the surrounding oceans, rests on a single large plate, extending 6,200 miles (10,000 km) from California to Iceland. A little plate that fits in next to it, off the coast of Washington State, is just 310 miles (500 km) wide. (For a map of the tectonic plates, see page 11.)

DID YOU KNOW?

The earth's tectonic plates move at about the same rate as your fingernails grow— an average of a little more than an inch (2.5 cm) per year.

The earth's tectonic plates do not fasten together solidly but float on upper parts of the mantle. Flowing movements in the mantle cause the plates to move about, sometimes pulling apart, or crashing into each other, or rubbing sideways along their edges. This is a very slow process—the plates move between ½ inch and 4 inches (1 and 10 cm) per year. But they are so massive that even these slow, creeping movements can cause momentous effects. Earthquakes may occur at the edges of moving plates that collide. Volcanoes can form where two plates move apart. And the edges of bumping plates may buckle and fold, building up mountain ranges. The discovery of all this was a long process, filled with errors along the way.

TWO

ON THE WAY TO A THEORY

Early explorers of the world drew maps of the lands they visited. These early maps were crude and often inaccurate. Nonetheless, some keen observers noticed that the various continents seemed to fit together like pieces of a jigsaw puzzle. For instance, the bulge on the east coast of South America appeared to fit nicely into a notch on the west coast of Africa. The Dutch mapmaker Abraham Ortelius was one of the first to notice this. In 1596 he commented about the fit of the coastlines in his book on geography, suggesting that the American continents had been "torn away from Europe and Africa . . . by earthquakes and floods." The English philosopher Francis Bacon wrote in 1620 that the fit between the coastlines of the continents on opposite sides of the Atlantic Ocean could be "no mere accidental occurrence," but he had no suggestions on what could have caused it. In 1750 the French naturalist Georges de Buffon wrote about the way South America and Africa fit together and proposed that perhaps at one time, in the distant past, these two lands were joined together. In 1858 the French geographer Antonio Snider-Pellegrini actually drew "before" and "after" maps showing how the American continents had once been joined to Europe and Africa. By that time, other kinds of evidence began to support this idea.

✦ PIECES OF THE PUZZLE ✦

In the early nineteenth century, the German explorer Alexander von Humboldt reported that the rocks of Brazil, on the east coast of South America, were quite similar to those of the Congo, in western Africa. Humboldt suggested that these lands were originally joined until a huge tidal wave carved out the Atlantic Ocean. More clues to the great "earth puzzle" were provided by naturalists who traveled between the continents and reported that the same species of turtles, snakes, and lizards could be found in both South America and Africa. They also found similar **fossils**, preserved remains of ancient life. Many similarities were also discovered between plant and animal species in Europe and North America. For example, fossils of camels were found in both North and South America, even though today they are found only in Africa. Some scientists speculated that land bridges used to connect all the continents until, in the recent past, such bridges sank into the seas.

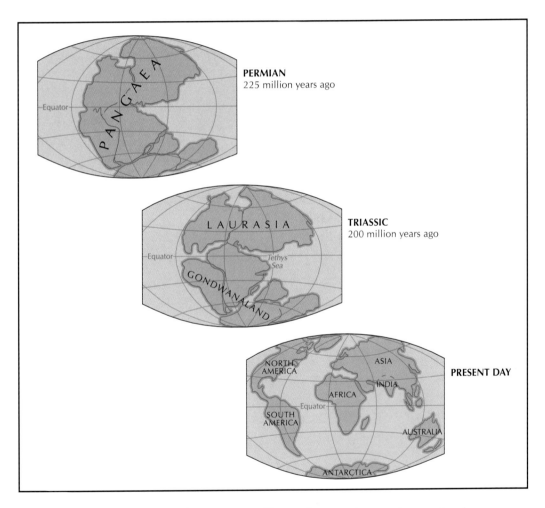

These maps depict how, over millions of years, the continents slowly "drifted" to their present positions. The drift is still going on.

Scientists offered many different theories to explain how the earth's continents were formed. Like Humboldt, some thought that sudden great catastrophes had broken apart large landmasses and formed the oceans. These theories supported the great floods described in the Bible and in the myths of people elsewhere. Other scientists thought the lands of the earth had gone through a series of slower, more gradual changes. Today, scientists believe that both catastrophes and slow, gradual processes have helped to shape the surface of our planet.

In 1885 Edward Suess, an Austrian geologist, published a work called *The Face of the Earth*. In it he proposed that in the distant past (about 180 million years ago) the continents were condensed into two giant landmasses: a southern area he called **Gondwanaland** and a northern one he named **Laurasia**. He suggested that Laurasia ultimately separated into Europe, Asia, and North America, while Gondwanaland gave rise to the rest of the continents.

A Lost Continent?

In the 300s B.C., the Greek philosopher Plato wrote about an ancient island in the west, Atlantis. It had been described by Egyptian priests as larger than Asia Minor and Libya combined. Atlantians were rich and powerful and had a brilliant civilization. But they became so greedy and corrupt that the gods punished them. In a single day and night, huge explosions shook the island, and Atlantis sank into the Atlantic Ocean. The story of Atlantis may have been just a myth, or a fable Plato made up to illustrate his philosophical ideas. For many centuries, though, Europeans speculated about "lost Atlantis" and sent out expeditions to look for it. The catastrophe theories of the late eighteenth and nineteenth centuries provided new fuel for believers in Atlantis. They thought that Atlantis was the part of Gondwanaland that sank when the Atlantic Ocean was formed.

In 1908 two American geologists, Frank Taylor and Howard Baker, independently proposed that the continents had moved during past ages. Taylor thought, for example, that the mountain ranges in Europe and Asia formed from the movement of the continents toward the equator. But since neither could offer any evidence to support their theory, they were not taken seriously.

Alfred Wegener, a German **meteorologist**, made important contributions to weather science; he was the first to use balloons to track air currents, for example. But today he is remembered most for proposing the theory of **continental drift**. In 1911 Wegener happened to read a scientific paper on the fossils of identical plants and animals that had been found in lands on opposite sides of the Atlantic Ocean. Instead of accepting the existing theory—that the continents had once been connected by land bridges—Wegener focused on the close fit between the coastlines of Africa and South America. He began to look for evidence that these continents had once been joined. For example, the layers of rocks in South Africa matched those of Brazil. Mountain ranges seemed to begin on one continent and continue on another, although separated by thousands of miles. The Appalachian Mountains in North America, for instance, matched up

Alfred Wegener, father of the theory of continental drift, is boring a hole into the arctic ice while on expedition.

neatly with the Highlands of Scotland. "It is just as if we were to refit the torn pieces of a newspaper by their matching edges," Wegener wrote. Another intriguing fact was that fossils in various places often showed that the climate in those regions had been quite different in the past. For instance, fossils of tropical plants had been found in Spitsbergen, an island in the cold Arctic Ocean that must once have been warm. Rock deposits from glaciers were present in India, Australia, Africa, and South America, suggesting that these warm areas must once have been in a cold climate, perhaps near the South Pole.

Wegener said that these findings could be explained if all the landmasses on the earth once had been joined together. He came up with a theory that about 300 million years ago, they formed a vast supercontinent, which he called **Pangaea** (from Greek words meaning "all the earth"). This supercontinent broke apart, like a cracked ice floe, and the pieces (today's continents) have been slowly drifting away from each other ever since. Wegener first presented his theory in a lecture in 1912, and then in a book, *The Origin of Continents and Oceans*, in 1915.

Like most new theories, the idea of continental drift was met at first by disbelief and even ridicule. Geologists of the time called it "ludicrous" and raised numerous objections. Wegener thought that the continents moved through the earth's crust like icebreakers plowing through ice sheets. Other scientists asked how the soft, light rocks of the continents could break through the hard, dense rocks of the ocean floor; the landmasses would soon have become distorted. And where did the energy to push the continents apart come from? Wegener thought that the earth's rotation on its axis, along with the gravitational pull of the sun and the moon, provided the energy for the movement. But these forces were too weak; one scientist calculated that a tidal force strong enough to move continents would stop the earth's rotation within less than a year! When Wegener died in 1930, at the age of fifty, most scientists still thought his theory was ridiculous.

✦ UNDER THE SURFACE ✦

Not everyone rejected Alfred Wegener's theory. Arthur Holmes, an English geologist, thought the continental drift idea seemed reasonable and should not be rejected just because Wegener had not explained what force was responsible for the movements. In 1929 Holmes suggested that the landmasses at the surface might be moving because of **convection currents** in the mantle beneath them. Though scientists of the time did not pay much attention to this suggestion, most scientists today believe that convection in the mantle plays an important role in the movements in the earth's crust.

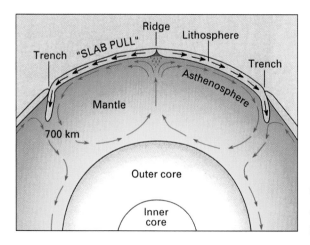

Convection currents in the mantle most likely play an important role in the movements in the earth's crust.

WHAT IS CONVECTION?

You may have noticed that when a pot of soup is heated, the liquid begins to bubble and churn. Pieces of vegetables, meat, and other solid particles rise to the surface and then disappear back into the boiling soup. The heat being applied to the bottom of the pot provides the energy for this movement. As the heated material gets farther from the heat source, it gradually cools. Eventually it falls and is replaced by new heated material. The circular flows of matter in a heated liquid are called convection currents. They help to distribute the heat throughout the liquid. Convection currents can also arise in air and other gases. They help to spread the heat from a radiator through the whole room. Convection currents in the atmosphere create winds.

In the late 1930s David Griggs, an American geologist, showed that seemingly solid rock can actually flow slowly if it is subjected to very high temperatures and pressures. In the decades that followed, other researchers found that some parts of the ocean floor contained much less sediment (solid matter that had settled to the bottom) than it should have if it were as old as the landmasses. And the oldest rocks that were found in the sea were about 200 million years old—much younger than the rocks on land. Much of this new evidence was provided by extensive exploration of the sea bottom in the efforts to track submarines during World War II. Further exploration of the oceans also revealed that the continents fit together even better if the outlines of the **continental shelves** (the relatively shallow-water areas just off the coast) are used instead of the outlines of the landmasses themselves.

Meanwhile, Emile Argand, a Swiss geologist, argued that the folded, buckled pattern of the **strata** (rock layers) in the Swiss Alps could best be explained if the mountains had been formed in a collision of continents. The South African geologist Alexander Du Toit, another firm believer in Wegener's theory, spent his life accumulating evidence to support the concept of continental drift.

For three decades after Wegener's death, the gradual buildup of evidence supporting his theory occurred beneath the surface of the main currents of geologic opinion. The supporters of his theory were just a small, scattered minority; the majority of scientists were still unconvinced. As one geologist had remarked at a 1928 meeting of the American Association of Petroleum Geologists, "If we are to believe Wegener's hypothesis, we must forget everything which has been learned in the last seventy years and start all over again."

✦ THREE ✦

THE PLATE TECTONIC THEORY

Studies in the 1950s produced some surprising new information about the earth—findings that could be explained only if it was assumed that the continents had moved about during the long history of our planet. This new support for Wegener's continental drift concept came from the study of the earth's natural magnetism.

✦ THE EARTH IS A MAGNET ✦

In the sixteenth century the English scientist William Gilbert correctly guessed that the earth acts like a huge magnet. That is why a compass needle always points to the North Pole. Gilbert could not explain how this happened. Today, we know that the magnetism is created by the flow of molten iron and nickel in the outer part of the earth's core. These metals are naturally magnetic, and their movements generate electric currents, which in turn produce a magnetic field that extends not only through the earth but also some 37,000 miles (60,000 km) out into space.

If a bar of a magnetic metal is suspended from a thread and allowed to move freely, it will move so that one end points toward the North Pole (in the arctic region) and the other end points toward the South Pole (in the antarctic region). The same thing happens to bits of metal in the rocks that form when

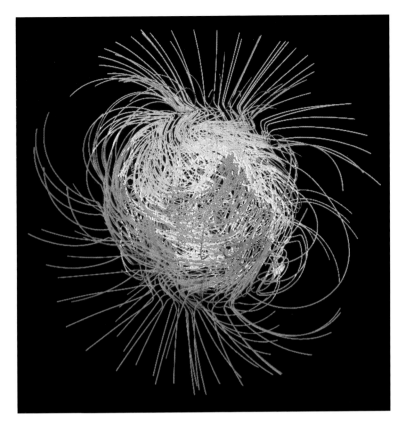

The flow of molten iron and nickel in the outer part of the earth's core is responsible for the earth acting like a giant magnet.

molten lava from a volcano cools and solidifies. These rocks are like compasses, showing the location of north and south.

When geologists examined rocks from older strata, however, they made a curious discovery. The magnets in these rocks do not point exactly toward the North Pole; and the more ancient the rocks, the farther they are from "true north." By comparing the magnetic alignment of rocks from different time periods, scientists in Europe found that about 250 million years ago the magnetic North Pole was apparently located in Hawaii. Later it wandered over to Japan, and finally it reached its present position in the Arctic. Observations of magnetic rocks in other continents also suggested that the North Pole had wandered over the ages. In each case it seemed to have traveled over a different path, from various other locations to its present place. How could the North Pole have been located in different places at the same times? That was impossible.

Another explanation fit the facts much better. Instead of assuming that the North Pole had moved around, what if it had stayed in the same place while the continents were moving? Geologists took another look at Wegener's continental drift theory. If the continents had been moving apart after splitting off from a big supercontinent, the alignment of magnetic rocks in various places on these continents would have changed over time. When the geologists plotted the positions of the moving continents at the times the magnetic rocks were formed, sure enough—the magnets in the rocks all pointed to the same North Pole.

✦ DEEP-SEA STORY ✦

Explorations of the ocean basins during the 1950s revealed a lot of intriguing new information. The ocean bottoms do not slope smoothly like a washbasin; their contours are just as varied as those of the continents, with huge underwater mountains, valleys, and canyons. A long mountain range, the Mid-Atlantic Ridge, was found in the middle of the Atlantic Ocean floor. Later it was discovered that similar mountain ranges are found in all the ocean bottoms. They form a long underwater ridge about 37,000 miles (60,000 km) long, winding around through the water-covered parts of the earth like the seam on a baseball. A deep canyon, or **rift**, runs down the middle of each **midocean ridge**, and these underwater mountain ranges are often shaken by earthquakes and volcanic **eruptions**. The rifts mark cracks in the earth's crust, where magma wells up from the mantle below and flows out continually as lava.

This computer-graphics rendering dramatically focuses on a portion of the seafloor of the Mid-Atlantic Ridge.

NATURE'S BAR CODES

Tests of rock samples taken from the midocean ridges have shown that the rocks closest to the center of the rifts are the most recently formed, and that the age of the rocks increases the farther they are from the rift on each side. When geologists plotted the magnetic alignment of the rocks, they were shocked to find that on each side of the rift the rocks form alternating bands whose magnetism is lined up exactly opposite to that of rocks in the next band. The bands are also symmetrical in position and width on either side of the rift. Today geologists believe that the earth's magnetic poles have reversed themselves every three million years or so. The exact time intervals between reversals have varied, so the alternating rock bands are of different widths—producing a pattern that looks very much like the bar codes used in supermarkets to record the names and prices of products.

Deep **trenches** also occur in various parts of the ocean floor, dropping sharply to depths 5 to 6 miles (8 to nearly 10 km) below the ocean surface. These trenches form a ring around the Pacific Ocean, along the western coasts of Central and South America and in midocean in the southwestern Pacific. There are also trenches in the Indian Ocean too, and even a few small ones in the Atlantic. These trenches are areas of frequent earthquake activity.

In 1959 the American geologist Harry Hess proposed a theory that he called **seafloor spreading** to account for these features of the ocean basins. He suggested that as the hot molten rock in the mantle slowly rises, it presses against the rock formations in the crust. When it reaches a weak spot, cracks form. The increased pressure causes the cracks to widen, allowing the hot magma to squeeze through. Finally it breaks through to the ocean floor as molten lava. The cold water cools the lava to hard rocks. Each successive flow adds another layer, slowly building up ridges on the ocean floor. The force of the upwelling material forces the ridge edges apart, and the seafloor slowly spreads.

If new material is continually being added to the earth's crust at the midocean ridges, is the earth getting larger? No, because older parts of the seafloor are continually being pushed down into the mantle at the deep trenches. So there is a kind of recycling process between the earth's crust and the mantle, where old crust is melted down and new crust forms when magma breaks through to the surface and solidifies.

Hess's theory of seafloor spreading provided what Wegener lacked: an explanation of *how* the continents could move through the earth's crust. In 1967, W. Jason Morgan, an American geologist, and Dan McKenzie, a British geologist, took the reasoning a step further. Each one independently suggested that the earth's surface is made up of a number of movable plates. In 1968 American geologists Bryan L. Isacks, Jack E. Oliver, and Lynn R. Sykes suggested that these solid plates can move because they float on the liquid mantle beneath them. The **plate tectonic theory** was complete.

PLATE TECTONICS IN ACTION

From 1968 to 1983, a ship called the *Glomar Challenger* sailed the world's oceans, as well as the Mediterranean and Red seas. Specially designed for oceanographic research, the ship drilled out more than 19,000 core samples from 624 sites on the sea bottom. These rock samples, each 30 feet (9 m) long and 2 $\frac{1}{2}$ inches (about 6 cm) in diameter, provided a wealth of knowledge about the earth's crust and its history. Since then, other ships have continued to explore the ocean bottoms. The samples they have brought back have provided more information on the age of the ocean floor. Studies of the samples from the magnetic anomalies have allowed scientists to calculate just how fast the seafloor was spreading (and how fast the continents were moving) at various times in the past.

Meanwhile, the use of satellites orbiting the earth has made it possible to measure exactly how fast the continents are moving *now*. The twenty-one satellites of the Global Positioning System (GPS), for example, continuously transmit radio signals back to the earth. Each GPS station on the ground compares signals from at least four satellites to determine its exact position relative to the other ground sites. From those data, its exact latitude, longitude, and elevation can be determined.

The results obtained in the past few decades have shown, among other things: The North Atlantic Ocean formed about 180 million years ago. Eurasia and North America are moving apart at about 1 inch (2.5 cm) a year. The fastest-moving place in the world is a region in the South Pacific near Easter Island, known as the East Pacific Rise. It is traveling more than 6 inches (15 cm) each year.

✦ HOW PLATE TECTONICS WORKS ✦

Geologists have mapped the regions of volcanic and earthquake activity and seafloor spreading. They have found that these regions form a network over the earth's surface, like the cracks on an eggshell that has been bumped but not broken open. This network outlines the irregular shapes of the plates that form the earth's crust. Actually, the plates also include the uppermost part of the mantle, which is cooler and more rigid than the rest of the mantle below it. Together the crust and uppermost part of the mantle form the **lithosphere** (from the Greek *lithos,* meaning "stone"). It is a rigid layer of rock, but—like an eggshell—is brittle and can crack, or **fracture**. The plates that form the lithosphere float on a hot, semisolid layer of mantle called the **asthenosphere** (from *asthenes,* the Greek word for "weak"). Under the action of high temperatures from below and the pressure from the lithosphere above it, acting over

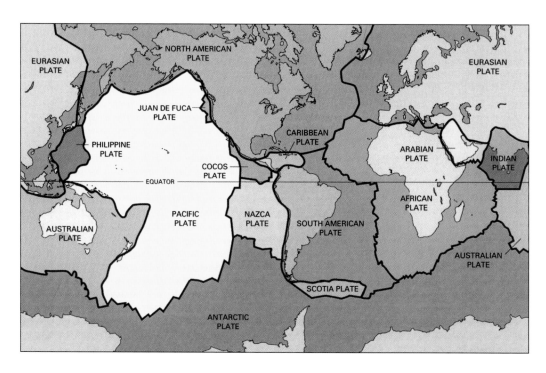

The outer part of the earth is broken into more than a dozen tectonic plates—rigid slabs—that are constantly moving.

long ages of time, this part of the mantle can soften and flow, allowing the plates floating on it to move.

The lithosphere averages about 50 miles (80 km) thick, but the parts under the oceans are much thinner than those that form the continents—less than 9 miles (15 km) for the youngest parts of the seafloor to about 125 miles (200 km) or more in mountainous parts of the continents. Why don't the thick continental plates sink into the asthenosphere? The reason is that they are made of much lighter rocks than the denser lithosphere under the oceans.

There are three main types of boundaries between tectonic plates:

- **divergent boundaries**, where the plates are moving away from each other and new crust is formed from mantle material.
- **convergent boundaries**, where plates moving toward each other bump. (If an oceanic and a continental plate collide, the denser oceanic plate dips under the edge of the other, and crust is melted down into mantle. If two continental plates collide, they buckle and form a mountain range.)
- **transform boundaries**, where plates are sliding past each other; no crust is destroyed, and no new crust is formed.

The plate movements at these boundaries can produce different effects, depending on what kind of plates are involved.

Most of the divergent boundaries are found under the oceans and result in seafloor spreading. This kind of movement produced the Atlantic Ocean, once just a little inlet between the Americas and Eurasia. Magma may ooze out slowly along the slit between the plates, producing new seafloor in the rifts between

Lava spurts through rifts in the ground surrounding Iceland's Krafla volcano.

As on land, most life in the seas depends on photosynthesis, the production of food by plants or plantlike algae, using the energy of sunlight. A variety of marine animals feed on these plants—or on each other. But the sun's rays cannot penetrate the great depths of the seafloor in most of the oceans, so there are few living things there. When scientists in deepwater diving vessels explored the areas near the midocean rifts, however, they discovered a whole new world full of life. In 1977 hot springs (called **geothermal vents**) were found on the Galápagos Rift, off the coast of Ecuador. A variety of unusual sea animals, including giant tube worms, huge clams, mussels, eyeless shrimp, miniature lobsters, and octopuses were thriving around these hot springs. (More than three hundred new species have been discovered in various thermal vent communities.)

Geothermal—or actually hydrothermal (since they are under water)—vents send up plumes of heated water that encourage an amazing growth of deep-ocean life.

What were they living on? Researchers found that bacteria living in the springs were able to use the chemical energy stored in sulfur compounds to produce food—without photosynthesis. It is now believed that these bacteria may be similar to the first life forms that developed on the ancient earth, before photosynthesizing plants added oxygen to our planet's atmosphere.

ridges. In some areas, the oozing magma may be concentrated in one spot, building up to form a volcanic island. (Other islands form during explosive eruptions.)

The Mid-Atlantic Ridge runs through Iceland, which lies at the boundary of the North American and Eurasian plates. This northern island country is thus a kind of natural "laboratory," where scientists can study changes on land similar to those that occur deep under the sea. Iceland has a number of active volcanoes, with cracks in the ground around them. Near one of them, called Krafla, new cracks appear every few months, and those already present keep widening. In the decade between 1975 and 1984, the ground shifted about 23 feet (7 m). Sometimes the rifting (cracking) is combined with volcanic activity. Just before each new eruption of the volcano, the ground rises 3 feet (1 m) or more, then suddenly falls.

EARTH'S NEWEST ISLAND

On November 14, 1963, fishermen about 25 miles (40 km) off the southwest coast of Iceland observed a volcanic eruption surging out of the water. Starting under water, about 425 feet (130 m) beneath the surface, it continued for three and a half years. During that time, the lava flowing out of the volcano gradually built up an island 1 square mile (2.6 square km) in area, with a peak more than 550 feet (168 m) above sea level. The island was named Surtsey, after Surtur, a giant in Norse myths who would set fire to the earth at the Last Judgment.

The island of Surtsey, off the coast of Iceland, was created dramatically in November 1963 by volcanic action in the Mid-Atlantic Ridge.

While the volcano was still erupting, Surtsey was declared a nature preserve, open only to scientists. British researchers photographed the eruption from airplanes, and teams of scientists made trips to the growing island to observe its development. In less than a year, flies and seagulls found the island. Seeds carried by the ocean currents and dropped by birds from nearby islands and from the coast of Iceland began to sprout; the first flowering plant appeared in 1965. In 1970 a bird was found nesting and raising its young in the warm lava. Since then life has continued to settle in. Fifty different plants have been found growing on Surtsey, and eight types of birds are now breeding on the island in the summers.

When two tectonic plates converge, their movement toward each other results in a *very* slow collision. What happens then depends on what kinds of plates are involved. If a passenger car collides with a big truck on the highway, the smaller car may slip under the truck's bumper and be crunched underneath the truck. Something like that may happen when an ocean plate collides with a continental plate. The edge of the thinner, denser ocean plate slips under the edge of the continental plate. Its greater weight pulls it down into the mantle. This process is called **subduction**. At the boundary a very deep, narrow trench is formed. As the edge of the continental plate rides up over the subducting ocean plate, huge mountain ranges may be thrust up. The Andes Mountains of South America formed in this way, as the South American Plate was lifted in a collision with the smaller Nazca Plate in the Pacific Ocean, along the Peru-Chile trench.

Subduction allows the size of the earth to remain the same, even while new crust is being formed by seafloor spreading. Some scientists now believe that this, rather than convection in the mantle, is the main driving force in plate tectonics. In 1994 Japanese geologist Seiya Uyeda stated at an international conference that subduction plays the major role in "shaping the earth's surface features" and "running the plate tectonic machinery." Under the action of gravity, the colder, denser ocean plate sinks into the trench, dragging the rest of the plate with it.

Subduction may seem like a smooth process, but it is usually accompanied by violent earthquakes. This happens because pieces of the colliding plates may crack, become wedged in place for a while, then move suddenly. Areas of convergence between ocean and continental plates may also produce active volcanoes. The huge trench that rings the Pacific Ocean is called the "Ring of Fire" because of the frequent volcanic eruptions and earthquakes that occur there.

When two ocean plates converge, usually one is subducted under the other, forming a trench. The Marianas Trench, the deepest in the world, was formed in a collision between the faster-moving Pacific Plate and the slower-moving Philippine Plate. Subduction between ocean plates produces underwater volcanoes, which may eventually build up into a curving chain of islands paralleling the curve of the trench. Earthquakes also occur as the plates converge.

DID YOU KNOW?

The deepest place in the world is in the Marianas Trench in the South Pacific. It dips 36,205 feet (11,035 m) below sea level. Compare that with the world's highest land mountain, Mount Everest in Asia, whose peak is only 29,028 feet (8,848 m) above sea level.

When two continental plates meet in a head-on collision, the results are spectacular. Both plates have about the same density, so neither one tends to be subducted under the other. Instead, they crunch together, and their edges buckle upward or sideways, producing huge mountain ranges. The Himalayas, the highest mountain range in the world, were produced about 50 million years ago, when the Indian Plate crashed into the Eurasian Plate and eventually became attached to Asia. In the original supercontinent Pangaea, India had been joined to what is now Africa. After the continents broke apart, the Indian Plate gradually drifted up to its present position. Fossils of sea creatures have been found atop the Himalayas—further evidence that these lands were once at the edge of the ocean.

When a car on the highway sideswipes another, the effects are much less dramatic than a head-on collision—but a lot of damage may still be done. When two tectonic plates slide past each other sideways, the area where they meet is called a transform boundary, a **strike-slip fault**, or a **fracture zone**. Usually they connect two zones of spreading (divergent plate boundaries) or two trenches (convergent plate boundaries). Most transform boundaries are in the

Vehicles drive along a road that cuts through the San Andreas Fault in California, where the Pacific and North American tectonic plates meet and have caused numerous earthquakes. The rock layers in the cliff have been twisted and folded by tectonic forces.

oceans, but a few are found on land. One famous example is the San Andreas Fault, which runs down two-thirds the length of California. At this boundary, the Pacific Plate is moving northwest and grinding against the North American Plate. This has been going on for 10 million years, at a rate of about 2 inches (5 cm) per year. Fracture zones are sites of shallow earthquakes, as the earth's crust continually adjusts for the shifts in position.

✦ CONTINENTS ADRIFT ✦

The movements of the tectonic plates have produced dramatic changes in the conditions on the continents. Scientists now believe that about 425 million years ago most of earth's landmasses were clustered in the southern half of the planet. North America and Europe were at the equator. By 250 million years ago, the landmasses had joined to form the supercontinent Pangaea. (For a map of continental drift, see page 11.) Then, around 200 million years ago, Pangaea began to break up. First it split across the middle, into a northern continent, Laurasia, and a southern landmass, Gondwanaland. About 135 million years ago, Gondwanaland began to split. Africa and South America gradually moved apart, forming the Atlantic Ocean, Australia became an island touching Antarctica, and India split off from Africa and began to drift northward, toward Asia. The splits continued. By about 65 million years ago, Laurasia was mostly separated into Eurasia and North America, but they were still joined in the far north by the landmass that is now the island of Greenland. When the split was completed, about 40 million years ago, Greenland had become an island. Meanwhile, Australia was beginning to move away from Antarctica.

The movements of the continents had some important effects on the animals, plants, and other creatures that lived on them. By about 225 million years ago, when Pangaea was still a single supercontinent, fish swam in the oceans, along with invertebrates such as crabs and clams, and a variety of plants and animals had begun to live on the lands. This was the start of the Age of Reptiles. Not only crocodiles, lizards, snakes, and other reptiles similar to the species of today but also giant dinosaurs were the dominant animals on land.

The first mammals were mouse-sized insect eaters. Around 190 million years ago, they appeared in Gondwanaland, the southern continent that had already separated from Laurasia—except for a land bridge between Africa and Eurasia at what is now the Strait of Gibraltar. The earliest mammals laid eggs, like their reptile ancestors. Their two surviving descendants are the duckbilled platypus and the spiny anteater (echidna), which today live only in Australia. The babies of later mammals developed—to a point—inside their mother's body. They were born while they were still very tiny and helpless, and managed to crawl into a special pouch on their mother's belly. There, safe and protected, they finished their development while feeding on milk produced by their mother's mammary gland. Over many years these primitive mammals, called **marsupials**, evolved into a great variety of species, of different sizes and habits. Some, such as opossums and koalas, were able to climb trees. Others, such as kangaroos and wallabies, became specialized for jumping with long, strong hind legs and a long tail that helped them to balance while sailing through the air. There were also marsupial "mice," marsupial "cats," marsupial "wolves," and many others.

The duckbilled platypus, which lives in Australia, is one of two surviving egg-laying mammals.

COMMUTER TURTLES

The continental drift theory has explained some puzzles of animal behavior. After sea turtles hatch from their eggs, they toddle down the beach and swim out into the ocean. The smell and taste of the water there make a deep impression on them, and years later when they mate and are ready to lay eggs of their own, the female turtles travel back to the same beach where they were born. Today, green sea turtles that live and feed off the coast of Brazil do not lay their eggs on the beaches there. Instead, they swim 1,250 miles (more than 2,000 km) to tiny Ascension Island in the middle of the Atlantic Ocean to make their nests. On this long voyage they do not feed, and they face many dangers. This seems puzzling until we recall that tens of millions of years ago, the Atlantic Ocean was a lot smaller and Ascension Island was right off the coast of Brazil. At that time it made sense for turtles feeding near the coast to swim across to a nearby island and lay their eggs where they would be safe from mainland predators. The trip got longer as the continents moved apart, but this happened very slowly (just a few centimeters each year) and the turtles had time to adapt. The lengthening trip helped to shape the turtles' evolution: Those with stronger flippers for swimming and heavier fat deposits to provide food along the way were more likely to survive and have offspring like themselves.

Marsupials were still the dominant mammals when Australia broke away from Gondwanaland. The island continent remained caught in a sort of "time warp," left behind when mammals on the mainland evolved further. **Placental mammals** appeared before the next continental splits; their young spent a much longer time developing inside the mother's body, nourished from her blood through an organ called the placenta. When they were born, they were much better equipped to survive, and in many areas competed successfully with marsupials for food and living space. Some marsupials did survive in Africa and South America, and opossums migrated up to North America over a land bridge. But placental mammals soon greatly outnumbered the marsupials, except in Australia. No placental mammals lived there until the first human settlers brought dogs, whose descendants are today's Australian dingoes. Later settlers introduced sheep, cattle, and rabbits.

Further tectonic movements explain some other peculiarities in the way certain types of mammals are distributed over the continents. There are monkeys in Asia, Africa, and South America, for example, but the Old World monkeys of

Asia and Africa are rather different from the New World monkeys that live in the South American jungles. The two lines developed in different ways after the split between South America and Africa was complete. Apes and our apelike ancestors developed from the Old World monkey line and never appeared in the Americas. Humans first migrated into North America from Asia about 30,000 years ago over a land bridge that existed for a while after Siberia and Alaska bumped together.

THE CIRCULAR TALE OF THE HORSE

We know from fossil records that in North America, about 60 million years ago, the first horses appeared. They were dog-sized animals with five-toed feet. Scientists have named them *Eohippus*, which means "dawn horse." Gradually horses grew larger and became more specialized for running. Meanwhile, they spread to Europe, Asia, and Africa while connections between the continents still existed. The present-day horse, *Equus*, developed by about 3 million years ago. During an ice age about 8,000 years ago, horses became extinct in North America, but they survived in the Old World. What about the mustangs, our "native wild horses"? They were brought to America from Spain by the conquistadores in the sixteenth century.

FIVE

VOLCANOES: EARTH'S SAFETY VALVES

"A dense black cloud was coming up behind us, spreading over the earth like a flood. Darkness fell as if the lamp had been put out in a closed room. The buildings were shaking as if they were being torn from their foundations. Ashes were falling hotter and thicker, followed by bits of pumice and blackened stones, charred and cracked by the flames. You could hear the shrieks of women, and the wailing of infants and the shouting of men. I had the belief that the whole world was dying and I with it until a yellowish sun finally revealed a landscape buried deep in ashes like snowdrifts."

This was the way seventeen-year-old Pliny the Younger, in a letter written in A.D. 79, described the eruption of Mount Vesuvius, a volcano in southern Italy. When the volcano began to erupt, panic spread through the nearby city of Pompeii. More than 90 percent of the inhabitants fled, but the rest refused to leave their homes. Rocks and ash rained down on the city, piling up at a rate of 6 inches (15 cm) per hour. Then, suddenly, a choking cloud of hot gases, ash, and rock poured out of the mountain at speeds up to 190 miles (300 km) per hour. No one in its path could escape. When the eruption ended, 19 hours after it began, the entire city of Pompeii was buried under a layer of ash 25 feet (8 m) deep. Nearly 1,800 years later, when archaeologists dug out the buried city, they found everything—houses, furniture, food, and the bodies of the volcano's 2,000 victims—perfectly preserved.

The volcanic eruption that wiped out Pompeii is one of the most famous in history, but it was not the most destructive. The eruption of Mount Pelée, on the Caribbean island of Martinique, in 1902, killed close to 30,000 people—nearly all the inhabitants of the nearby port city of St. Pierre—within minutes. One of the largest eruptions ever recorded was that of Mount Tambora on an island in Indonesia in 1815. Before the mountain "blew its top," with the power of millions of nuclear bombs, it was 14,000 feet (4,300 meters) high. In the eruption, a total of 12 cubic miles (50 cubic km) of magma poured out and fell over an area of more than 193,000 square miles (500,000 square km) of islands

These ruins, along a street at the site of the Roman city of Pompeii (in southern Italy), are stark monuments to the destructive volcanic activity of Mount Vesuvius, in the background.

and surrounding sea; the height of the mountain was decreased by nearly 4,600 feet (1,400 m), and instead of a cone, its top ended in a hollowed-out crater more than 4 miles (7 km) wide and nearly 2/3 of a mile (1 km) deep. The explosion itself and the huge **tsunamis**—sea waves—that it produced killed about 10,000 people. Another 82,000 died as a result of famine and disease in the following years because the thick ash deposits had buried all the fertile croplands in the area.

If volcanoes are so dangerous, why are people willing to live near them? One reason is that most volcanoes do not erupt very often. A volcano may stay quiet, or **dormant** (from the French word for "sleeping"), for hundreds or even thousands of years. (A volcano is considered **active** if it has erupted since written records have been kept. A volcano that is not expected ever to erupt again is classified as **extinct**.) There may not be any traditions or even myths among the people in the area to suggest that a particular volcano might be a threat, and even today there is no way to predict reliably when a dormant volcano is going to erupt. Meanwhile, people tend to settle in areas near volcanoes because the soil there is very fertile. Past flows of lava and ash are rich in minerals that were brought up from the interior of the earth. In fact, certain crops, such as the cacao tree that gives us chocolate and cocoa, grow best in volcanic soils.

THE YEAR WITH NO SUMMER

The eruption of Mount Tambora in 1815 affected not just the local area but the whole world. Clouds of dust and gases covered the earth for years, partly blocking out the sunlight. In 1816 snow fell during the summer months in many parts of the United States and Europe. That frigid time was known as "the year without a summer."

Ancient peoples thought volcanic eruptions were due to fires; even in the eighteenth century, many scientists thought they were caused by burning coal deposits underground. Now it is known that they are actually the result of plate tectonic processes that start deep within the earth's mantle.

The term *volcano* refers to both the opening, or **vent**, from which lava flows and the cone-shaped mountain that surrounds it. The mountain itself is the result of lava flows during past eruptions.

ATLANTIS REVISITED

Scholars today believe that if there really was an Atlantis—not just a myth invented or retold by Plato—it was an island called Thera in the Aegean Sea, about 70 miles (110 km) north of Crete. According to ancient Egyptian records, an enormous volcanic eruption destroyed Thera around 1500 B.C. The series of earthquakes and tsunamis that accompanied the eruption wiped out the flourishing Minoan civilization on Crete, which was the major power in the area at that time.

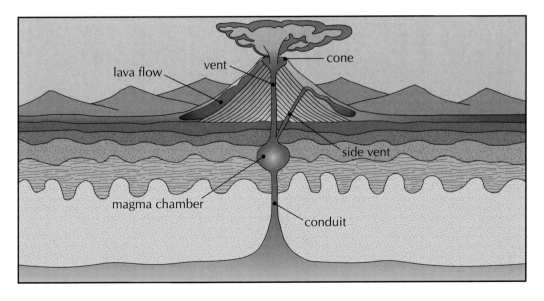

This diagram shows a simplified side view of a volcano.

A volcano starts down in the mantle, where temperatures are 1,100°–2,200°F (600°–1,200°C), hot enough to melt rocks. Where there are gaps or cracks in the rocks of the crust, hot magma may ooze upward. It tends to rise because it contains dissolved gases and is lighter than the rocks. Melting the surrounding rock, the magma may accumulate, forming a giant **magma chamber** under the surface. Finally it breaks through and bursts out in an eruption.

CAUTION: CONTENTS UNDER PRESSURE

Have you ever noticed a warning on a bottle or can of soda? If you have ever shaken one before opening it, you know why the warning is there. When the container is opened, the high pressure on the carbon dioxide gas dissolved in the soft drink is suddenly reduced and it expands rapidly. Bubbly soda explodes out all over everything. That is similar to what happens when a volcano erupts. While it is still trapped under rock, the hot magma is also under great pressure. When it reaches the surface, that pressure is suddenly removed. That is why a huge cloud of hot gas, ash, and rocks may shoot up into the air when a volcano erupts.

There are about two dozen volcanic eruptions each year on land and many more under the oceans. Most of the world's volcanoes are found along boundaries where tectonic plates are bumping together or moving apart. Some, such as the Hawaiian Islands, are in the middle of tectonic plates. They are parts of a chain of volcanic mountains strung out in the middle of the Pacific Ocean, nearly 2,000 miles (3,200 km) from the nearest plate boundary. Some of the volcanoes are extinct, but others have been active for quite a long time.

After the plate tectonic theory was developed, scientists wondered why these volcanoes did not seem to fit into the theory. In 1963, J. Tuzo Wilson, a Canadian geologist, proposed an explanation. He suggested that deep in the mantle there are certain small, long-lasting, exceptionally hot regions. These **hotspots** rise through the mantle in the form of **thermal plumes** and heat the portion of the plate just above them, melting rock and forming a volcano. Thus, the Hawaiian Islands were formed as the Pacific Plate slowly moved over a hotspot deep in the mantle. Over long ages of time this hotspot produced one volcano after another. Each one erupted for a while, gradually building up a mountain high enough to rise above sea level and produce an island, then became extinct as the plate moved past the hotspot and a new volcano formed farther down the chain.

✦ WHAT COMES OUT OF A VOLCANO ✦

When a volcano erupts, it releases a mixture of red-hot magma, ash, and gases. If the mixture contains a lot of gas, it bursts out violently, blasting the magma into particles and forming a tall cloud as the gases expand rapidly under the lower pressure of the atmosphere. Scientists call this violent type of eruption a **Plinian eruption**, after Pliny the Elder, a natural scientist who died in Pompeii. He was the uncle of Pliny the Younger, whose eyewitness description of the eruption, preserved by the Roman historian Tacitus, opened this chapter. The eruption cloud may collapse suddenly, turning into a deadly **pyroclastic flow** that speeds down the mountain, destroying everything in its path. (*Pyroclastic* comes from Greek words meaning "broken by fire.")

A river of lava destroys a visitors' center in Hawaii as it makes its way relentlessly toward the ocean.

Dante Alighieri, a thirteenth-century Italian poet, wrote *The Inferno,* an account of an imagined trip down into Hell. So when a robot was built to explore the fiery interior of volcanoes, it seemed natural to name it Dante II. Samples of the hot gases released in volcanic eruptions can provide valuable information, but collecting them is a very dangerous job. In 1993, for example, eight volcanologists were killed during on-the-spot studies of erupting volcanoes. In 1994 the robot Dante II was able to explore the Mount Spurr volcano in Alaska, even descending down the steep crater walls to gather gas samples from the crater floor. Space researchers from NASA (National Aeronautics and Space Administration) hope someday to use robots like Dante II to explore the harsh, barren terrains of other planets.

The lava that flows out of a volcanic vent may be thin and runny or thick and gooey, depending on how much silica, the mineral that forms sand, it contains. Lava with very little silica flows rapidly, like a glowing red-hot river, and may spread out over great distances. Lava with a large content of silica is thick and sticky and oozes slowly. Generally it cools into solid rock before it has moved very far; in fact, this kind of lava may actually solidify inside the volcano's opening, forming a plug. A plugged volcano may later explode, when a new buildup of magma blows out the plug; or it may calm down and become extinct. In some very old extinct volcanoes, the outer part of the mountain has been worn away so that only the plug remains.

Lavas may contain chemicals that give them various colors. **Basalt**, for example, is a dark-colored lava, either black or dark gray. **Rhyolite** is light-colored, from white to pale gray, greenish, pink, or tan. The lava in Yellowstone National Park is rhyolite.

In addition to lava, volcanic eruptions release rocks and large amounts of gas, dust, and ash. The gas is mostly steam, but there are usually large amounts of carbon dioxide, sulfur dioxide, and other gases as well. The gases released by very explosive volcanic eruptions may shoot up high into the stratosphere, up to as much as 30 miles (50 km) above the earth's surface, and remain there for several years. **Volcanic bombs** (baseball- or even basketball-sized rocks formed by drops of lava that have solidified) usually fall close to the vent. **Ash** (lava broken into fine particles) and **cinders** (coarser lava particles) cover a larger area, and the finest particles (**volcanic dust**) can be carried by the winds all around the world. Some of the ash may fall into streams near the volcano and form **mudflows**. These can be very destructive, flowing over nearby villages at up to 60 miles (nearly 100 km) per hour.

When magma makes its way up toward the surface, it may pass nearby underground streams or springs. The hot rock is much hotter than the boiling point of water, 212°F (100°C), so the heated water may turn into steam and explode out of the ground, shooting in a hot fountain high into the air. Such hot springs, called **geysers**, are found in some areas of volcanic activity. The most famous is Old Faithful, in Yellowstone National Park. Named for its unusually regular eruptions, which occur about every 74 minutes, Old Faithful has not missed a scheduled eruption in the more than 120 years it has been recorded.

"Old Faithful" dwarfs visitors in Yellowstone National Park who have come to watch the geyser blow its top.

✦ KINDS OF VOLCANOES ✦

Depending on the way volcanoes erupt, they can produce a number of different kinds of structures besides the familiar cone-shaped mountains.

In **flood eruptions**, runny lava may spread out for hundreds or even thousands of miles (kilometers). The lava flows may erupt from many different cracks in the earth's crust over a large area. Instead of forming a mountain, this kind of eruption builds up a large plain or plateau. The Columbia River Plateau, which covers much of Oregon, Washington, and Idaho, was built up in this way. It extends over an area of 100,000 square miles (nearly 260,000 square km).

Many volcanoes have the shape of a broad dome. These are called **shield volcanoes**. They are formed when lava flows out of the vent and cools as it flows over the surrounding area. As more eruptions send out lava flows, each successive layer builds on the one before it until a dome-shaped mountain forms. Shield volcanoes are among the largest in the world. Most of the Hawaiian Islands are shield volcanoes.

Cinder-cone volcanoes are formed from the accumulation of cinder and ash that is released by each eruption. As this material falls back close to the vent, it forms a cone-shaped mountain. A **crater** is often found at the top of the cone. This is a bowl-shaped hollow, formed when explosive blasts blow material away from the vent. The Sunset Crater in Arizona is an example of a cinder-cone volcano.

*This peaceful scene is Crater Lake, Oregon, a giant caldera—
the collapsed magma chamber of a volcano.*

Composite volcanoes are formed from alternating layers of thick, sticky lava and volcanic ash, produced in repeated eruptions. Some of the tallest cone-shaped mountains, such as Mount Fuji in Japan, are of this type.

Sometimes the magma chamber beneath a volcano may become empty. The full weight of the soil and rocks above may make the chamber collapse, to form a large crater called a **caldera**. Rains or water flows may fill this crater, forming a lake. Crater Lake, in Oregon, is a giant caldera. It is 6 miles (nearly 10 km) across and almost 2,000 feet (about 600 m) deep.

✦ SIX ✦

EARTHQUAKES AT FAULT

Suddenly the ground shook. Hundreds of thousands of people were wakened from their sleep. Their buildings were trembling. Roads ripped open, swallowing cars like tiny toys. Gas lines snapped, starting thousands of fires throughout the city. Buildings swayed, then came crashing to the ground. People raced into the streets, shivering with fear.

The place was Kobe, Japan. The date: January 17, 1995. An earthquake had devastated the city. Although the tremors lasted only 12 seconds, more than 5,500 people died. In addition, more than 190,000 buildings were destroyed or badly damaged, leaving more than 300,000 people homeless. The docks of the city, one of the most active seaports in the world, were almost completely destroyed. The Japanese government had to spend close to $150 billion to repair the damage in Kobe. Devastating as it was, however, the Kobe earthquake was far from the worst in history. In fact, the Great Kanto earthquake, which hit Japan in 1923, killed 143,000 people in Tokyo and the nearby area. The 1976 Tangshan earthquake in the Hebei Province of China killed more than 250,000 people!

Earthquakes as severe as the one that struck Kobe strike somewhere on the earth every few years. But most of them do not occur near large cities, so the loss of life and property is not so great.

Earthquakes are powerful, the biggest ones thousands of times stronger than the first atomic bombs dropped at the end of World War II. Large earthquakes

*Cyclists casually pedaling along a street in Kobe, Japan,
provide a sharp contrast to rescue workers searching a building
severely damaged by an earthquake measuring 7.2 on the
Richter scale the day before.*

cause more damage than tornadoes, hurricanes, or floods. Nearly a million earthquakes occur each year, but most of them occur deep within the earth and can be detected only by scientific instruments.

✦ WHAT CAUSES EARTHQUAKES ✦

Most earthquakes are the result of movements of the earth's tectonic plates and occur along **faults**, the boundaries between moving plates. Nearly half of all earthquakes occur in subduction zones, areas where two plates moving toward each other collide and the edge of one plate slips under the edge of the other. The deepest earthquakes occur in subduction zones. Most of them occur in the Ring of Fire, the arc of deep trenches that curves around the Pacific Ocean. It is also known as the Circum-Pacific belt. (A long area of frequent earthquake activity is called a **belt**.) Another earthquake zone, the Alpide belt, passes

Earthquakes come suddenly and can have terrible effects, so people living in areas where quakes are frequent have always looked for explanations. Many ancient peoples believed that earthquakes were a punishment for something they had done to displease the gods. The ancient Greeks, for example, believed that Poseidon, the god of the sea, caused earthquakes when he was angry with the mortals on earth. According to another Greek myth, the giant Atlas held the earth on his shoulders. When he got tired and moved his shoulders, an earthquake occurred. The Japanese, living on volcanic islands in an earthquake zone, thought a catfish held the world on its back. A god was assigned to watch it, but sometimes his attention wandered and the fish wriggled, shaking the earth. Other ancient peoples believed that the earth was held up by giant pigs, turtles, oxen, or snakes. In each case, they believed that an earthquake occurred when the animals moved.

In the fourth century B.C., the Greek philosopher and scientist Aristotle looked for a more scientific explanation. He thought that violent winds, trapped beneath the earth's surface, sometimes burst out, producing an earthquake. This theory influenced scientists' beliefs for more than 2,000 years.

through the Mediterranean region (including Greece, Italy, and Turkey) and eastward through the Indian Ocean to meet up with the Circum-Pacific belt in southern Asia. Earthquakes also occur at transform boundaries, or strike-slip faults, where two plates are moving sideways past each other. The most famous is the San Andreas Fault in California. The great San Francisco earthquake of 1906 resulted from movement along this fault. The earthquakes that occur at strike-slip faults are shallower than those in subduction zones.

Moving plates in contact exhibit **friction**, a resistance to the movement that is caused by rough spots on their surfaces catching against each other. Friction generates a lot of energy. (You can demonstrate this on a much smaller scale by rubbing the palms of your hands against each other. Within seconds you will feel the heat build up.) As the tectonic plates continue to rub against each other, friction locks them in place for awhile, but stresses build up. Eventually the plates break free, releasing the stresses and producing an earthquake. Some parts of the San Andreas Fault zone move slowly and steadily. This kind of movement, called **creep**, produces frequent small or moderate earthquakes. In other parts of the

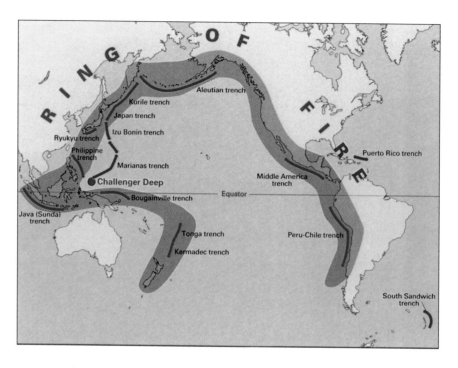

There's nothing pacific (peaceful) about the Ring of Fire,
a huge belt of volcano and earthquake activity that nearly
surrounds the Pacific Ocean.

fault, portions of the plates get locked together for tens or hundreds of years while stresses build up, then produce devastating earthquakes.

Earthquakes can also occur at divergent boundaries, such as the midoceanic ridges where plates are moving apart and seafloor spreading is occurring. These earthquakes are often associated with volcanic activity. Volcanic earthquakes can also occur within tectonic plates, far from their edges. Such earthquakes, which are usually rather small, generally occur just before and during volcanic activity. These quakes are caused by the pressure exerted on rock structures as magma forces its way toward the surface from cavities deep within the earth. For example, in the weeks before Mount St. Helens in Washington State erupted in May 1980, there were many minor earthquakes.

Other earthquakes within tectonic plates occur in areas where the ground is soft and may be under great stress from temperature and pressure changes in the rocks beneath. The three powerful earthquakes that struck New Madrid, Missouri, in 1811 and 1812 were quakes of this kind. They caused the Mississippi River to change its course and were felt 1,000 miles (1,600 km) away.

Human activities can also cause earthquakes. When a new dam is built, huge amounts of water build up behind towering walls. This puts a great deal of pressure on a relatively small area. If a fault is nearby and rocks are already under stress, the added pressure may cause them to slip. Earthquakes have occurred in the areas of the Hoover Dam in the United States, the Aswan High Dam in Egypt, and a number of others. Large nuclear explosions, set off underground, have led to earthquakes. So has the pumping of wastes or other fluids deep into the ground. Earthquakes occurred, for example, when waste fluids from the city of Denver, Colorado, were pumped into deep wells east of the city. After the pumping was stopped, the earthquakes soon stopped also.

✦ WHAT HAPPENS DURING AN EARTHQUAKE ✦

As stresses build up at a boundary between two colliding tectonic plates, the rocks begin to bend and bulge. Like a stretched rubber band, rocks can absorb a certain amount of stress. But eventually they break or slip into a new position, setting off vibrations in the earth's crust.

The place where the rocks break or move is called the **focus** of the earthquake. It is usually deep underground—from dozens to hundreds of miles (kilometers) below the surface. The spot on the surface directly above the focus is called the **epicenter** of the earthquake. It is there that the most severe damage usually occurs. The vibrations, called seismic waves, spread out from the focus in all directions.

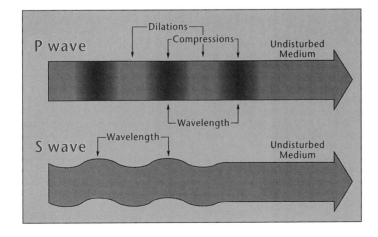

P waves and S waves are two different ways that energy from earthquakes can move through a solid.

There are two main types of seismic waves: **body waves** and **surface waves**. The faster body waves move through the earth, while the slower surface waves travel along the surface. Most earthquake damage is caused by the body waves. There are two types of body waves. The faster ones are called **P waves** or **primary waves** because they are the first to arrive at any point in the vicinity of an earthquake. They compress and stretch the earth's crust, like the movement in a Slinky toy. The second, slower, type, are known as **S waves** or **secondary waves**. They produce side-to-side or up-and-down movements, like ocean waves or the snakelike wave produced by shaking one end of a stretched rope. This movement is perpendicular to the movement of the P waves and is called **shearing** motion. As the body waves travel underground, away from the focus, the P waves cause the rocks to be pushed and pulled. Buildings rocked by these waves shake back and forth. Since P waves are faster, they arrive first. They are followed by the S waves, which cause rocks and buildings to move from side to side, in a shearing motion.

Surface waves are the last to arrive. People feel them as slow, rocking movements. Despite the frightening feeling, they cause little damage. Most earthquakes last for less than 15 seconds, but rare ones may go on for a minute or more. The main shock in the Lisbon, Portugal, earthquake of 1755 was felt for six minutes.

A number of large earthquakes are preceded by one or more rather minor tremblings called **foreshocks**. Following the main earthquake, there are often additional rather minor quakes called **aftershocks**. They follow immediately after the main earthquake and may continue for days or even longer. Generally, aftershocks cause less damage than the main earthquake. But sometimes, if an aftershock is close to a heavily populated area, it may cause more damage than the main event. Aftershocks are often due to the fact that only part of the strain built up in the rocks was released by the main earthquake. Additional movement of the rocks to relieve the rest of the built-up stresses produces the aftershocks.

Most of the destruction during a major earthquake is caused by the shaking and trembling ground. The severe stresses created by these motions can collapse many structures that have not been reinforced enough to make them earthquake-proof. Avalanches and landslides can also cause damage, burying whole villages. In cities broken gas lines or flammable items shaken down onto hot stoves can start fires that sweep through whole neighborhoods. Broken water lines may hamper the efforts of the firefighters.

Since most big earthquakes are associated with faults located near the ocean, another destructive force is often unleashed. Powerful ocean waves called tsunamis can form. Earthquakes that occur on the ocean floor can send out pow-

The great earthquake at Lisbon, Portugal, in 1755 produced huge tsunamis, as this German engraving of the time depicts.

erful waves through the water and up to the surface that cause the nearby ocean waters to swell. While still at sea, tsunamis may be only 2–3 feet (0.6–0.9m) high. A ship might pass over one and not notice it at all. But as these **seismic sea waves** approach the shore, they can build up to enormous heights—100 feet (30 m) or more. These giant waves can stretch for hundreds of miles, and they can travel as fast as a jet plane, at speeds exceeding 500 miles (800 km) per hour. Tsunamis are often so powerful that they can move many miles inland and flood villages and towns on the way. Most of the 60,000 people who died from the Lisbon earthquake in 1755 were drowned by the tsunami that followed it.

Made in Japan

It is appropriate that *tsunami* is a Japanese word. Japan has had more than its share of them—at least fifteen devastating tsunamis in the past three hundred years. The worst was a seismic sea wave that killed more than 27,000 Japanese in 1896. Japan is in an especially active earthquake zone because it lies at the intersection of three tectonic plates.

Earthquakes occur every day somewhere within the earth. Indeed, dozens occur every hour throughout the year. Most of them are so faint that even the best instruments do not detect them, but many thousands are detected each year. Using seismographs, scientists known as **seismologists** detect, measure, and study earthquakes. Some seismographs can detect the seismic waves that form when rocks move beneath the earth, even ones that have formed thousands of miles away. Others contain devices called **tiltmeters** that can detect tiny earth movements in the focal region that may signal an oncoming earthquake. When seismic waves are detected, a seismograph produces wavy lines that are recorded as a **seismogram**. Today seismograms may be recorded on paper, magnetic tape, film, or computer.

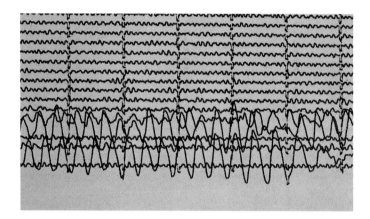

This modern seismogram shows recordings of the January 1995 earthquake in Kobe, Japan—made in Columbia, California!

Two different scales are used to measure earthquakes. The **Richter scale** assigns a number rating on a scale of 0 to 9, indicating the earthquake's power, or magnitude. The higher the number, the more powerful the earthquake. An earthquake with a magnitude of 1 to 2 can be detected only by instruments. (There are more than 500,000 earthquakes of this strength each year.) At a Richter magnitude of 3 to 4, hanging lights sway and there may be minor damage. (From 10,000 to 100,000 earthquakes of this magnitude occur each year.) At magnitude 5 to 6, dishes, books, or other objects may fall off shelves and walls of buildings may crack. (These earthquakes happen 20 to 200 times a year.) Up to ten earthquakes with a magnitude of 7 to 8 occur each year. These are the "big ones" that can make buildings collapse and cause highways and bridges to buckle and twist. Because there is such a great range in the size of earthquakes, the Richter scale uses mathematical expressions called logarithms. With each higher whole number on the scale, the power of the earthquake goes up ten-fold. A magnitude 7 earthquake, for example, is 10 times as strong as a magnitude 6 quake. A magnitude 8 quake is a million times as strong as one with a magnitude of 2. (Richter magnitude refers to the size of the waves, but the energy involved goes up even faster. So a magnitude 7 quake releases more than 30 times as much energy as a magnitude 6 earthquake.) The **Mercalli scale** measures earthquakes in terms of their effects, rather than their power. In its 12-point scale, a rating of 3 points corresponds to a barely noticeable earthquake, while an earthquake with a Mercalli intensity of 10 points causes major damage to buildings, overpasses, and other structures.

THE FIRST SEISMOGRAPH

A Chinese scientist named Chang Heng invented an instrument for detecting earthquakes back in A.D. 132. A pendulum in the center was attached to a ring of twelve dragon heads, each of which held a bronze ball in its mouth. Twelve statues of toads with open mouths sat directly below the dragons. If an earthquake occurred, the first tremors set the pendulum swinging, and a ball dropped from one of the dragons into the mouth of the toad beneath it. The device also indicated the location of the earthquake: The toad that caught the ball was the farthest from the epicenter.

In areas with frequent earthquakes, seismographs set up in various locations are used in efforts to predict when new quakes will occur. In addition to changes in the seismic waves, there are other clues: Water levels shift suddenly. Radon gas is released from rocks in the area. Animals behave unusually—for example, dogs bark wildly for no apparent reason; ducks leave their ponds; caged birds fly against the sides of their cages; and fish rise to the surface in great numbers or orient themselves all in the same direction like the swimmers in a water ballet. Earthquake prediction is still far from an exact science, however. Although some successful predictions have saved thousands of lives by having people evacuate cities where quakes were expected to occur, the same techniques have failed to predict other earthquakes or have forecasted quakes that never happened.

SEVEN

PLATE TECTONICS AND THE FUTURE

Some geologists predict that someday the California coast will snap off at the San Andreas fault and drift into the Pacific Ocean. For a while that portion of California will be an island, they say, but eventually it will disappear into the deep trench off Alaska in the Aleutian Islands chain. Other experts argue, however, that this won't happen because the San Andreas Fault is only about 9 miles (15 km) deep, a quarter of the thickness of the earth's crust in that area—not enough to cause such a split. Moreover, the low density of the continental crust on which California sits keeps it floating high in the mantle, like an iceberg rising high above the surface of the ocean.

HEADING FOR CALIFORNIA

Satellite measurements suggest that Australia is currently moving toward California. Of course, it is not expected to get there very soon, since it is moving at a pace of about 2 inches (5 cm) per year as a rift in the Indian Ocean gradually widens. Within a few million years, moreover, Australia's progress will be slowed and its direction shifted by the huge Pacific Plate that lies southwest of California.

Geologists do agree, however, that the Atlantic Ocean widens each year, while the Pacific Ocean continues to narrow. Eventually, the North American continent may merge with Asia as Alaska slowly crunches into Siberia. Meanwhile, Africa will drift northward, squeezing the Mediterranean Sea into a narrow channel. Because of rift lakes that are widening, East Africa may split off from the mainland, creating a new sea. Of course, all these things will take a hundred million years or more to happen. What effects and applications will plate tectonics have for the near future, within the lifetimes of people living today?

✦ CAN EARTHQUAKES AND VOLCANIC ERUPTIONS BE PREDICTED? ✦

In 1975 Chinese seismologists correctly predicted that an earthquake was about to strike in Haicheng. Officials ordered the evacuation of the cities and villages in the area, and 90,000 people left their homes. Two days later, an earthquake measuring 7.3 on the Richter scale destroyed nine out of ten buildings in the area, but not a single person died. The following year, however, earthquake struck in Tangshan, a major industrial center in northern China with a population of more than 1 million. It caught everyone unaware. More than 250,000 people died in that quake.

In 1965 Japan set up a five-year plan to develop earthquake prediction methods. Now in its seventh five-year plan, that country has spent a total of $1.3 billion on the effort—and has not yet successfully predicted any earthquakes. The program has concentrated especially on the Tokai region southwest of Tokyo, where three tectonic plates meet and there has not been a major earthquake since 1854. Figuring Tokai was overdue for a magnitude 8 earthquake—a "big one"—seismologists set up underground strain meters all over the area, as well as four seismic stations equipped with tiltmeters on the nearby seabed. A total of 186 measurements are made each day and transmitted to computers in Tokyo. So far there has not been an earthquake in Tokai, and some scientists are questioning whether the program is worth the expense.

In fact, Robert J. Geller, an American geologist who is a professor at the University of Tokyo, has recently suggested that earthquake prediction might actually be impossible. There are just too many factors involved, many of which cannot be measured. It is likely that scientists will keep on trying to develop prediction methods, however. There is too much at stake in terms of lives and property that could be saved by reliable forecasts.

Scientists have found evidence that some gigantic volcanic eruptions—at least twenty times as large as the 1980 eruption of Mount St. Helens—occurred in past ages. In fact, one of them, which spewed out about 400,000 cubic miles (1.7 million cubic km) of lava (320,000 times as large as the Mount St. Helens eruption) in Siberia around 250 million years ago, may have had a devastating effect on life on earth. Around that time, according to the fossil evidence, up to 95 percent of all the marine species became extinct—perhaps because of changes in climate due to the huge amounts of particles the eruptions sent into the atmosphere.

Today, a huge volcanic eruption could have a devastating effect on the world's human population. An eruption at Yellowstone, for example, could deposit up to an inch (3 cm) of ash on places as far away as New York City, Boston, and Montreal. The ash would black out television, radio, and telephone signals. Collapsing power lines and clogged generators would shut down electric power systems, and volcanic dust in the air would stall the engines of jet planes. From geological evidence, we know that the last major eruption at Yellowstone occurred about 600,000 years ago, and the two before that at intervals of 800,000 and 600,000 years apart. So we could be due for another "big one" any time now.

✦ POWER FROM THE DEPTHS ✦

In human terms, the energy contained in the hot lava that pours out of an erupting volcano is "wasted." But we do have some ways to tap the heat energy stored in the magma beneath the earth's crust. This heat energy is referred to as **geothermal energy**.

Hot springs are one source of geothermal energy that has been used by people for thousands of years. The ancient Romans had bathhouses that were heated by nearby hot springs. Today, in Iceland, Japan, and other parts of the world, the water from hot springs is used to heat homes and various other buildings. Geothermal energy can also be used to produce electricity. The heat is used to turn water into steam, which then is used to turn a turbine that drives a generator.

To get at the hot areas below the surface, engineers must drill. The temper-

ature goes up about 54°F (30°C) for each 0.6 mile (1 km) the drill descends. In some parts of the world—usually where tectonic plates are colliding—molten rock is near the surface. Water piped down a hole that has been drilled into the rock becomes superheated and turns into steam, which rises and is used to generate electricity. In most places geothermal energy is too expensive to compete with other power sources. But as we use up our supplies of fossil fuels such as coal and oil, the plentiful source of energy trapped inside the earth will probably be used more and more.

Geothermal vents—hot springs—in Iceland not only produce heat and electricity for home and industry but provide residents with a warm lake to swim in.

✦ PLATE TECTONICS ON OTHER WORLDS ✦

Is Earth the only tectonically active world in our Solar System? Observations made by spacecraft suggest that volcanoes probably played an important role on the Moon and Mercury at one time, but they lost their internal heat more rapidly than the larger Earth, and have been inactive for the last billion years. High concentrations of sulfur measured in the atmosphere of Venus by the Pioneer Venus spacecraft in 1979 decreased over the next few years. This may be an indication of a huge volcanic eruption. Radar images of Venus sent back by the Magellan spacecraft beginning in 1990 showed volcanoes and also long, curving valleys similar to the oceanic trenches on our

DID YOU KNOW?

The Man in the Moon—the features of the "face" that people see in the moon when it is almost full—is actually made up of volcanic craters and dark flows of lava.

This close-up of the "Man in the Moon," taken by the Apollo 13 space mission, shows some of the moon's many craters.

planet. Mars apparently does not have tectonic plates, although it did have active volcanoes at one time. Olympus Mons on Mars is the largest volcano in the solar system. A cone-shaped mountain 18 miles (29 km) high and 372 miles (nearly 600 km) wide, it may have continued to erupt for a billion years. Signs of volcanic activity and perhaps of tectonic processes have been observed on two of Jupiter's moons, Io and Ganymede.

Volcanic eruptions allow some of a planet's internal heat to be released, and heat is radiated out into space. This is a slow but continuing process on our dynamic Earth. Eventually, like the Moon, Mercury, and Mars, Earth will have lost so much of its internal heat that convection in the mantle—and the tectonic processes that shape and reshape our planet's surface—will cease. But scientists have calculated that billions of years will pass before that happens. In the meantime, the pattern of continents and oceans will continue to shift and change, affecting the lives of all Earth's creatures.

Glossary

active volcano—a volcano that is currently erupting or has recently erupted.

aftershocks—minor (usually) tremors that follow a large earthquake.

ash—lava broken into fine particles.

asthenosphere—the semisolid portion of the mantle beneath the lithosphere.

basalt—a type of rock consisting of dark-colored lava.

belt—a long area of frequent earthquake activity.

body waves—fast-moving seismic waves that spread through the earth.

caldera—a large bowl-shaped depression formed when an empty magma chamber collapses or the top of a volcano is blown off during a violent eruption.

cinder-cone volcano—a cone-shaped mountain formed by repeated eruptions in which cinders and ash accumulate close to the vent.

cinders—lava broken into particles (coarser than ash particles).

composite volcano—a cone-shaped volcano formed by alternating layers of lava and ash.

continental drift—the theory that the earth's continents have slowly moved apart after splitting off from a single supercontinent, Pangaea.

continental shelf—the shallow-water area just off the coast of a landmass.

continents—the large landmasses of the earth.

convection currents—circulation due to the upward movement of the heated portions of a gas or a liquid.

convergent boundaries—boundaries between tectonic plates that are moving toward each other (colliding).

core—the innermost part of the earth.

crater—a bowl-shaped hollow at the top of a volcano that forms when matter is lost during an eruption.

creep—slow, steady movement of tectonic plates at a transform boundary.

crust—the outermost (surface) layer of the earth.

divergent boundaries—boundaries between tectonic plates that are moving apart.

dormant volcano—a volcano that appears inactive but is capable of erupting.

earthquake—a trembling or shaking of the ground due to vibrations in the earth's crust caused by sudden movements of tectonic plates.

epicenter—the spot on the surface directly above an earthquake's focus.

eruption—a sudden, violent outburst; the ejection of molten rock, steam, or other matter from a volcano or geyser.

extinct volcano—a volcano that last erupted a long time in the past and is not considered capable of erupting again.

fault—a break in a body of rock; the boundary between moving tectonic plates.

flood eruption—the release of thin, runny lava that can spread out over great distances.

focus—the place where rocks break or move, producing an earthquake.

foreshocks—minor tremors that occur before a large earthquake.

fossils—preserved remains of ancient life.

fracture—a break or crack.

fracture zone—a transform boundary between two tectonic plates sliding past each other.

friction—the resistance to movement of two moving surfaces rubbing against each other, or the rubbing of two moving surfaces in contact, generating heat.

geologist—a scientist who studies the earth, its composition, and processes of movement.

geothermal energy—the internal heat of the earth.

geothermal vents—underwater hot springs on the ocean floor.

geyser—a hot spring that sends up fountainlike jets of water and steam into the air.

Gondwanaland—the southern supercontinent believed to have existed in the past.

hotspots—small, long-lasting regions deep in the mantle that are exceptionally hot.

Laurasia—the northern supercontinent believed to have existed in the past.

lava—the melted rock that comes out of an erupting volcano, or the rock formed when this solidifies.

lithosphere—the outermost layer of the earth, consisting of the crust and the upper part of the underlying mantle; it is composed of tectonic plates.

magma—hot, melted rock beneath or within the earth's crust.

magma chamber—a hollowed-out cavity beneath the surface of the earth's crust in which magma accumulates.

mantle—the layer of the earth between the crust and the core.

marsupials—primitive mammals whose young are born at a very immature stage and complete their development in a pouch on the mother's abdomen; most of the world's marsupials live in Australia.

Mercalli scale—a system for measuring earthquakes' effects.

meteorologist—a scientist who studies weather and climate.

midocean ridge—long underwater mountain ranges found at areas of divergence that run through the Atlantic, Pacific, and Indian Oceans.

mudflow—a combination of lava and water that can be very destructive.

Pangaea—a large supercontinent into which all the landmasses of the earth are believed to have been joined about 300 million years ago.

placental mammals—mammals whose young develop inside the mother's uterus and are nourished from her blood through an organ called the placenta.

plate tectonic theory—the theory that the earth's crust is made up of movable plates of rock.

Plinian eruption—a violent volcanic eruption in which lava explodes out of the vent and a cloud of hot gases and solid particles forms above it.

P waves (primary waves)—the fastest body waves, which stretch and compress rocks in the earth's crust.

pyroclastic flow—a mixture of lava and hot gases that may flow rapidly down a volcanic mountain after a Plinian eruption.

rhyolite—a type of rock consisting of light-colored lava.

Richter scale—a system for measuring earthquakes' power, or magnitude.

rift—a canyon or valley, especially the gap along the middle of midocean ranges.

seafloor spreading—the formation of new ocean bottom where two tectonic plates are moving apart.

seismic sea waves—tsunamis.

seismic waves—vibrations transmitted through the earth during an earthquake.

seismogram—a recording of the waves detected with a seismograph.

seismograph—an instrument that measures the vibrations transmitted through the earth during an earthquake.

seismologist—a scientist who detects, measures, and studies earthquakes.

shear—the tendency of a force applied to a solid, such as a rock stratum, to cause bending or breaking parallel to the force.

shield volcano—a volcano with the shape of a low, broad dome, formed by repeated flows of lava.

stratum (*plural* strata)—a layer, especially of rocks in the earth's crust.

strike-slip fault—a transform boundary between two tectonic plates sliding past each other.

subduction—a process at the boundary of two colliding tectonic plates in which one plate is drawn down or overridden by the other.

surface waves—slower-moving seismic waves that spread along the earth's surface.

S waves (secondary waves)—slower body waves that produce a shearing movement, up and down or sideways, perpendicular to the direction of the P waves.

tectonic plates—the approximately fifteen large masses of rock that make up the earth's crust.

thermal plumes—regions of exceptionally hot magma that rise through the mantle.

tiltmeter—a device that can detect tiny earth movements.

transform boundaries—boundaries between tectonic plates that are sliding past each other.

trench—a long, narrow depression in the sea floor, where subduction occurs.

tsunami—an unusually large ocean wave produced by an earthquake or undersea volcanic eruption.

vent—the opening in a volcano from which lava erupts.

volcanic dust—lava broken into very fine particles.

volcanic bombs—rocks formed from solidified lava that fall close to the vent.

volcano—an opening in the earth's crust through which hot matter escapes from the mantle below; or the cone-shaped mountain formed around such an opening by the buildup of lava and ash.

FOR FURTHER INFORMATION

BOOKS

Aylesworth, Thomas G., *Moving Continents: Our Changing Earth*. Springfield, NJ: Enslow, 1990.

Ballard, Robert W., and Walter Cronkite, *Exploring Our Living Planet*. Washington, DC: National Geographic Society, 1994.

Farndon, John, *How the Earth Works*. Pleasantville, NY: Reader's Digest Association, 1992.

Kious, W. Jacquelyne, and Robert I. Tilling, *This Dynamic Earth: The Story of Plate Tectonics*. Washington, DC: U.S. Geological Survey, 1996. [The complete book is also available free on the Internet.]

Planet Earth. Alexandria, VA: Time-Life Books (Student Library), 1997.

Sattler, Helen R., *Our Patchwork Planet: The Story of Plate Tectonics*. New York: Lothrop, Lee & Shepard, 1995.

INTERNET RESOURCES

http://205.147.23.131/eqpapers/00000072.htm Rand B. Schaal, University of California, Davis, "An Evaluation of the Animal-Behavior Theory for Earthquake Prediction" [a statistical analysis of evidence that animal behavior can predict earthquakes]

http://bang.lanl.gov/solarsys/earth.htm Calvin J. Hamilton, "Earth Introduction" [text and color illustrations on earth science including plate tectonics and volcanoes]

http://home.earthlink.net/~diblanc/tectonic/ptABCs.html Donald L. Blanchard, "The ABCs of Plate Tectonics" [extensive text on plate tectonics, plus link to another article, "Formation of Pangaea: The Making of a Supercontinent"]

http://gbms01.uwgb.edu/~dutchs/202ovhds/platec.htm Steven Dutch, "Continental Drift and Plate Tectonics" [outline of notes for a class at University of Wisconsin - Green Bay, with color diagrams]

http://maas-neotek.arc.nasa.gov/Dante/dante.html "Dante II Frame Walking Robot" [description of the Dante II robot and its exploration of the Mount Spurr volcano, with color photos]

http://pangaea.org/wegener.htm Patrick Hughes, "The Meteorologist Who Started a Revolution" [biography of Alfred Wegener and his continental drift theory]

http://pcsel10.scu.edu/jshiau/coen296/old.html "Old Faithful" [photos and text on the geysers at Yellowstone]

http://pubs.usgs.gov/gip/hawaii/ Robert J. Tilling, Christina Heliker, and Thomas L. Wright, "Eruptions of Hawaiian Volcanoes: Past, Present, and Future" [online edition of book published by U.S. Geological Survey, with color photos]

http://pubs.usgs.gov/publications/msh/ Robert J. Tilling, Lyn Topinka, and Donald A. Swanson, "Eruptions of Mount St. Helens: Past, Present, and Future" [online edition of book published by U.S. Geological Survey, with color photos]

http://pubs.usgs.gov/publications/text/dynamic/html W. Jacquelyne Kious and Robert I. Tilling, "This Dynamic Earth: The Story of Plate Tectonics" [online edition of the book published by the U.S. Geological Survey, with color photos and diagrams]

http://quake.wr.usgs.gov/ "Earthquake Information from the USGS" [maps and lists of recent earthquakes, how to prepare, earthquake information, contacts, and links]

http://seawifs.gsfc.nasa.gov/OCEAN_PLANET/HTML/ps_vents.html Dawn Stover, "Creatures of the Thermal Vents" [article about life around undersea thermal vents, from Smithsonian Institution Ocean Planet exhibition]

http://sizzle.thetech.org/exhibits_events/online/quakes/ "Earthquakes" [hypertext sequence on earthquakes by the Tech Museum of Innovation]

http://tqd.advanced.org/3669/3669/history.html "Who Invented the Theory of Continental Drift?" [history of the continental drift theory, plus experiments and activities]

http://ucaswww.mcm.uc.edu/geology/crest/lesplans/Contpuz.htm "The Continent Puzzle: Putting It All Together" [junior high lesson plan prepared in Southwest Ohio Professional Development Center—1995 Summer Institute, with links to information and activities]

http://visearth.ucsd.edu/VisE_Int/platetectonics/platetect.html "Geology: Plate Tectonics" [text and diagrams of plate tectonics, continental drift, and seafloor spreading]

http://volcano.und.nodak.edu/vw.html "Volcano World" [information on volcanoes of the world (and other worlds), activities for kids, lesson plans for teachers]

http://volcano.und.nodak.edu/vwdocs/vwlessons/lessons/lesson.html Scott Johnson, "Earth Science Lessons" [lessons and activities on plate tectonics, continental drift, earthquakes, and volcanoes, developed for and tested by students in grades 5–8]

http://windows.engin.umich.edu/ "Windows to the Universe" [text and animated color illustrations on plate tectonics, continental drift, volcanoes, and mountain building]

http://www.aist.go.jp/GSJ/~jdehn/vjump.htm "Volcanic Jump Station" [alphabetical list of hundreds of links to sites about volcanoes]

http://www.dartmouth.edu/~volcano/ "The Electronic Volcano" [maps, photographs, and text on active volcanoes; links to journals, observatories, and current events]

http://www.eqe.com/publications/kobe/kobe.htm "The January 17, 1995 Kobe Earthquake" [description of the effects of the Kobe earthquake]

http://www.eyjar.is/eyjar/eruption.html "Volcanic Eruption on Surtsey" [text and photos on the new island]

http://www.hcrhs.hunterdon.k12.nj.us/science/ptech.html "Plate Tectonics: Piecing Together the Earth" [materials on continental drift, plate tectonics, volcanoes, and earthquakes; web site prepared by students at a New Jersey high school]

http://www.isgs.uiuc.edu/isgsroot/dinos/earthsci_links.html

"Earth/Geoscience Information on the WWW" [links to over 1,000 sites, by category, prepared by the Illinois State Geological Survey Library]

http://www.kaibab.org/geology/contdrft.htm "The Grand Canyon and Continental Drift" [color maps of the continents at seven time periods from 550 million years ago to the present, with information on the wildlife at the Grand Canyon at those times]

http://www.muohio.edu/tectonics/ActiveTectonics.html "Active Tectonics" [outline of initiative to promote multidisciplinary research on active tectonic environments and animated graphics]

http://www.seismo.unr.edu/ftp/pub/louie/class/100/plate-tectonics.html J. Louie, "Plate Tectonics, the Cause of Earthquakes" [text, diagrams, and color photos (most from NASA)]

http://syzygyjob.com/rqlinks.shtml "Syzygy Earthquake Links" [links to earthquake maps and live seismograph displays from various parts of the world]

http://www.ucmp.berkeley.edu/geology/tectonics.html "Plate Tectonics" [animated graphics of the last 750 million years, text about the history and mechanisms of plate tectonics, references, links]

http://www.ucmp.berkeley.edu/history/wegener.html "Alfred Wegener (1880–1930)" [biography and photo of Wegener, discussion of his continental drift theory, color map of Pangaea, ocean floor images, and links to plate tectonics sites]

http://www.wdcb.rssi.ru/IDNDR/spitak/impact/colpredpi/sc00105a.html "Biological Precursors" [discussion of reports of unusual animal behavior before the Spitak earthquake in Russia in 1989]

INDEX